Our outward life requires them not—

Then wherefore had they birth?

—Mary Howitt

Excerpts: Mary Howitt, "The Use of Flowers;" Percy Bysshe Shelley, "The Sensitive Plant;" John Keats, "Ode on a Grecian Urn;" Rudyard Kipling, "The Children's Song" from *Puck of Pook's Hill*, copyright © 1906 by Macmillan and Co.; Charles Dickens, "The Ivy Green;" Gerard De Nerval, "Vers Dores;" Caroline Giltinan, "A Portrait;" John Keats, "Endymion;" Anonymous, "Lovers in the Garden" from *The Thousand and One Nights*; John Milton, *Paradise Lost*; William Wordsworth, "Intimations of Immortality;" William Blake, "Auguries of Innocence;" James Thomson, "Spring (The Seasons);" Beaumont and Fletcher, "The Rose;" Seneca, "De Beneficiis;" William Shakespeare, "Troilus and Cressida;" and Bliss Carmen, "Heaven."

The publisher has made a thorough effort to locate all persons having any right or interest in material presented in this book and to secure all necessary reprint permissions. If any required acknowledgements have been omitted or any rights overlooked, we regret the error and will correct the oversight in future editions of the book.

Designed by Marilyn Appleby, Natalie Hamilton, and Karina Ivanetich.
Edited by Jane M. Brown.
Photography copyright © 1990 by Alexandra K. Scott. All rights reserved. This book, or any portions thereof, may not be reproduced or transmitted in any form or by any means, electronic or mechanical, including photocopying, recording, or by any information storage and retrieval system, without permission in writing from the publisher.
Photography may not be reproduced without permission of Alexandra K. Scott.
ISBN 0-943231-29-9
Printed and bound in Singapore by Tien Wah Press Ltd.

Published by Howell Press, Inc., 700 Harris Street, Suite B, Charlottesville, Virginia 22901. Telephone (804) 977-4006.
First Edition

HOWELL PRESS

The National Cathedral Garden Address Book

Photography by Alexandra K. Scott

A Garden for the Ages

Situated within the 57-acre grounds of the Cathedral of Saint Peter and Saint Paul in Washington, D.C., the Bishop's Garden blossoms with history. Its oldest plantings date back to 1813, the year when Joseph Nourse, Registrar of the U.S. Treasury, purchased the land on which the garden now grows. He named the property Mount Alban in memory of a place he knew as a child growing up in England.

In 1898, five years after the Protestant Episcopal Cathedral Foundation was created by an act of Congress, Henry Yates Satterlee, the first Bishop of Washington, acquired Mount Saint Alban as the site for the cathedral. Mr. Satterlee then established Cathedral Park Board, with Beatrix Jones Farrand as landscaping consultant. Between 1907 and 1928, the Olmsted Brothers design firm handled the cathedral's landscaping.

Construction of the cathedral began in 1907, and as the building took shape, thoughts turned toward care of the burgeoning grounds. In 1916 Florence Brown Bratenahl, wife of the first dean of the cathedral, was asked to organize a garden guild to provide for "the care and beautification of the cathedral close." The first project undertaken by her newly formed All Hallows Guild was the development of the Bishop's Garden. Mrs. Bratenahl obtained the services of Frederick L. Olmstead, who designed a traditional English church garden.

Money to fund the Bishop's Garden came from garden club donations, All Hallows Guild membership dues, and memorial gifts. Florence

Bratenahl also donated a substantial amount of her own money to the project. By 1925 she had raised sufficient funds for work to begin, and within three years the major plantings of the Bishop's Garden were in place. When Mr. Olmstead left in 1928, Mrs. Bratenahl became the cathedral's landscape designer and remained in the position until 1936.

Since its inception, the Bishop's Garden has developed into a dazzling showcase of plants and flowers. Atlas Cedars in the Norman Court and the Glastonbury Thorn trace their origins to the Holy Land. Boxwood in the Hortulus derives from an old maze on Hayfield Manor, a property once owned by George Washington. Some of the ivy found in the garden was cut from World War I trenches the day the peace treaty that ended the conflict was signed. Other ivy was clipped from Thomas Jefferson's Virginia home, Monticello.

Structures within the Bishop's Garden also have historical origins. The 51 Pilgrim Steps in the eastern corner of the garden were built of sandstone from George Washington's Aquia Creek quarry. A twelfth-century carriage arch and fifteenth-century bas-relief of the crucifixion decorate the Norman Court. In the Hortulus stands a ninth-century French baptismal font, surrounded by monastic kitchen and infirmary herbs of types specified on a plant list kept by Charlemagne in 812 A.D.

Born of the vision of several talented and dedicated individuals, the Bishop's Garden today thrives as a living tribute to history. A haven for peace and solitude, it fulfills the vision of its creators, who endeavored from the beginning to plant "a garden for the ages."

Lily of the Valley.

The naiad-like lily of the vale,
Whom youth makes so fair, and passion so pale,
That the light of its tremulous bells is seen
Through their pavilions of tender green;
Percy Bysshe Shelley

Name _____
Address _____
_____

Phone _____

Name _____
Address _____
_____

Phone _____

Name _____
Address _____
_____

Phone _____

Name _____
Address _____
_____

Phone _____

Name _____
Address _____
_____

Phone _____

A

Name
Address
_____
Phone

Name
Address
_____
Phone

Name
Address
_____
Phone

Name
Address
_____
Phone

Name
Address
_____
Phone

A

Name

Address

Phone

Name

Address

Phone

Name

Address

Phone

Name

Address

Phone

Name

Address

Phone

Hortulus and Shadow House.

B

Name _____
Address _____
_____

Phone _____

Name _____
Address _____
_____

Phone _____

Name _____
Address _____
_____

Phone _____

Name _____
Address _____
_____

Phone _____

Name _____
Address _____
_____

Phone _____

B

Name

Address

Phone

Name

Address

Phone

Name

Address

Phone

Name

Address

Phone

Name

Address

Phone

B

Name

Address

Phone

Name

Address

Phone

Name

Address

Phone

Name

Address

Phone

Name

Address

Phone

Iris Germanica.

*B*eauty is truth, truth beauty,...

John Keats

Name _____
Address _____

Phone _____

Name _____
Address _____

Phone _____

Name _____
Address _____

Phone _____

Name _____
Address _____

Phone _____

Name _____
Address _____

Phone _____

C

Name
Address

Phone

Name
Address

Phone

Name
Address

Phone

Name
Address

Phone

Name
Address

Phone

C

Name
Address

Phone

Name
Address

Phone

Name
Address

Phone

Name
Address

Phone

Name
Address

Phone

English bronze sundial and Herb Bed.

*T*each us delight in simple things,
And mirth that has no bitter springs.

Rudyard Kipling

D

Name

Address

Phone

Name

Address

Phone

Name

Address

Phone

Name

Address

Phone

Name

Address

Phone

D

Name _____
Address _____
_____
Phone _____

Name _____
Address _____
_____
Phone _____

Name _____
Address _____
_____
Phone _____

Name _____
Address _____
_____
Phone _____

Name _____
Address _____
_____
Phone _____

D

Name

Address

Phone

Name

Address

Phone

Name

Address

Phone

Name

Address

Phone

Name

Address

Phone

Herb Cottage and old-fashioned Shrub Roses.

E

Name

Address

Phone

Name

Address

Phone

Name

Address

Phone

Name

Address

Phone

Name

Address

Phone

E

Name

Address

___

Phone

Name

Address

___

Phone

Name

Address

___

Phone

Name

Address

___

Phone

Name

Address

___

Phone

E

Name

Address

Phone

Name

Address

Phone

Name

Address

Phone

Name

Address

Phone

Name

Address

Phone

Herb Cottage Garden fountain.

*F*ast he stealeth on, though he wears no wings,
And a staunch old heart has he:
How closely he twineth, how tight he clings…
A rare old plant is the ivy green.

Charles Dickens

F

Name _____
Address _____
_____
Phone _____

Name _____
Address _____
_____
Phone _____

Name _____
Address _____
_____
Phone _____

Name _____
Address _____
_____
Phone _____

Name _____
Address _____
_____
Phone _____

F

Name _____
Address _____
_____
Phone _____

Name _____
Address _____
_____
Phone _____

Name _____
Address _____
_____
Phone _____

Name _____
Address _____
_____
Phone _____

Name _____
Address _____
_____
Phone _____

F

Name

Address

Phone

Name

Address

Phone

Name

Address

Phone

Name

Address

Phone

Name

Address

Phone

Rose Garden rose.

Each flower is a soul opening out to nature.
   Gerard De Nerval

G

Name

Address

Phone

Name

Address

Phone

Name

Address

Phone

Name

Address

Phone

Name

Address

Phone

G

Name

Address

_____

Phone

Name

Address

_____

Phone

Name

Address

_____

Phone

Name

Address

_____

Phone

Name

Address

_____

Phone

G

Name

Address

Phone

Name

Address

Phone

Name

Address

Phone

Name

Address

Phone

Name

Address

Phone

Woodland Path.

H

Name

Address

Phone

Name

Address

Phone

Name

Address

Phone

Name

Address

Phone

Name

Address

Phone

H

Name _____
Address _____
_____
Phone _____

Name _____
Address _____
_____
Phone _____

Name _____
Address _____
_____
Phone _____

Name _____
Address _____
_____
Phone _____

Name _____
Address _____
_____
Phone _____

H

Name _____

Address _____

_____

Phone _____

Name _____

Address _____

_____

Phone _____

Name _____

Address _____

_____

Phone _____

Name _____

Address _____

_____

Phone _____

Name _____

Address _____

_____

Phone _____

Climbing Roses.

Like a dear old lady
Dressed in soft brown cashmere
Sitting with quiet, folded hands, content
and peaceful
And smiling a mysterious promise,
My winter garden waits.

Caroline Giltinan

I

Name

Address

Phone

Name

Address

Phone

Name

Address

Phone

Name

Address

Phone

Name

Address

Phone

I

Name

Address

Phone

Name

Address

Phone

Name

Address

Phone

Name

Address

Phone

Name

Address

Phone

I

Name
Address

Phone

Name
Address

Phone

Name
Address

Phone

Name
Address

Phone

Name
Address

Phone

Celtic Cross and White Quince

J

Name

Address

Phone

Name

Address

Phone

Name

Address

Phone

Name

Address

Phone

Name

Address

Phone

J

Name

Address

Phone

Name

Address

Phone

Name

Address

Phone

Name

Address

Phone

Name

Address

Phone

J

Name

Address

Phone

Name

Address

Phone

Name

Address

Phone

Name

Address

Phone

Name

Address

Phone

Monarch butterfly on Michaelmas Daisies.

A thing of beauty is a joy for ever:
Its loveliness increases; it will never
Pass into nothingness.

John Keats

Name _____
Address _____
_____
Phone _____

Name _____
Address _____
_____
Phone _____

Name _____
Address _____
_____
Phone _____

Name _____
Address _____
_____
Phone _____

Name _____
Address _____
_____
Phone _____

K

Name

Address

___

Phone

Name

Address

___

Phone

Name

Address

___

Phone

Name

Address

___

Phone

Name

Address

___

Phone

K

Name _____

Address _____

_____

Phone _____

Name _____

Address _____

_____

Phone _____

Name _____

Address _____

_____

Phone _____

Name _____

Address _____

_____

Phone _____

Name _____

Address _____

_____

Phone _____

Shag Bark Hickory and North Rose Window.

Let us stay in the garden
Under gold palms
And dream.
Anonymous

L

Name

Address

Phone

Name

Address

Phone

Name

Address

Phone

Name

Address

Phone

Name

Address

Phone

L

Name

Address

Phone

Name

Address

Phone

Name

Address

Phone

Name

Address

Phone

Name

Address

Phone

L

Name _____
Address _____
_____
Phone _____

Name _____
Address _____
_____
Phone _____

Name _____
Address _____
_____
Phone _____

Name _____
Address _____
_____
Phone _____

Name _____
Address _____
_____
Phone _____

Peonies, Upper Perennial Border.

When God showered the earth;
so lovely seemed
That landscape…
John Milton

M

Name

Address

Phone

Name

Address

Phone

Name

Address

Phone

Name

Address

Phone

Name

Address

Phone

M

Name _____
Address _____
_____
Phone _____

Name _____
Address _____
_____
Phone _____

Name _____
Address _____
_____
Phone _____

Name _____
Address _____
_____
Phone _____

Name _____
Address _____
_____
Phone _____

M

Name

Address

Phone

Name

Address

Phone

Name

Address

Phone

Name

Address

Phone

Name

Address

Phone

Weeping Cherry and Norman Arch.

N

Name

Address

Phone

Name

Address

Phone

Name

Address

Phone

Name

Address

Phone

Name

Address

Phone

Name _____
Address _____
_____
Phone _____

Name _____
Address _____
_____
Phone _____

Name _____
Address _____
_____
Phone _____

Name _____
Address _____
_____
Phone _____

Name _____
Address _____
_____
Phone _____

N

Name _____
Address _____
_____
Phone _____

Name _____
Address _____
_____
Phone _____

Name _____
Address _____
_____
Phone _____

Name _____
Address _____
_____
Phone _____

Name _____
Address _____
_____
Phone _____

Peonies and Tulips.

Splendour in the grass,
—glory in the flower.
William Wordsworth

Name _____
Address _____
_____
Phone _____

Name _____
Address _____
_____
Phone _____

Name _____
Address _____
_____
Phone _____

Name _____
Address _____
_____
Phone _____

Name _____
Address _____
_____
Phone _____

Name _____
Address _____
_____
Phone _____

Name _____
Address _____
_____
Phone _____

Name _____
Address _____
_____
Phone _____

Name _____
Address _____
_____
Phone _____

Name _____
Address _____
_____
Phone _____

O

Name

Address

Phone

Name

Address

Phone

Name

Address

Phone

Name

Address

Phone

Name

Address

Phone

English bronze sundial on thirteenth-century Gothic capital.

To see a World in a Grain of Sand
And a Heaven in a Wild Flower
Hold Infinity in the palm of your hand
And Eternity in an hour

William Blake

P

Name

Address

Phone

Name

Address

Phone

Name

Address

Phone

Name

Address

Phone

Name

Address

Phone

P

Name

Address

Phone

Name

Address

Phone

Name

Address

Phone

Name

Address

Phone

Name

Address

Phone

P

Name

Address

Phone

Name

Address

Phone

Name

Address

Phone

Name

Address

Phone

Name

Address

Phone

Asters, Coreopsis, and Wind-flowers, Upper Perennial Border.

Infinite numbers, delicacies, smells,
With hues on hues expression cannot paint,
The breath of nature, and her endless bloom.
James Thomson

Q

Name

Address

Phone

Name

Address

Phone

Name

Address

Phone

Name

Address

Phone

Name

Address

Phone

Q

Name

Address

Phone

Name

Address

Phone

Name

Address

Phone

Name

Address

Phone

Name

Address

Phone

Q

Name

Address

Phone

Name

Address

Phone

Name

Address

Phone

Name

Address

Phone

Name

Address

Phone

Roses.

*O*f *all flowers,*
Methinks a Rose is best…

Beaumont and Fletcher

R

Name

Address

Phone

Name

Address

Phone

Name

Address

Phone

Name

Address

Phone

Name

Address

Phone

R

Name

Address

Phone

Name

Address

Phone

Name

Address

Phone

Name

Address

Phone

Name

Address

Phone

R

Name

Address

Phone

Name

Address

Phone

Name

Address

Phone

Name

Address

Phone

Name

Address

Phone

Shadow House.

S

Name

Address

Phone

Name

Address

Phone

Name

Address

Phone

Name

Address

Phone

Name

Address

Phone

S

Name

Address

Phone

Name

Address

Phone

Name

Address

Phone

Name

Address

Phone

Name

Address

Phone

S

Name
Address

Phone

Name
Address

Phone

Name
Address

Phone

Name
Address

Phone

Name
Address

Phone

Tulips and bas-relief of saints and martyrs by American sculptor George Gray Bernard.

Mary, Mary,
Quite contrary,
How does your garden grow?
With silver bells,
And cockle shells,
And pretty maids all in a row.
Traditional

T

Name

Address

Phone

Name

Address

Phone

Name

Address

Phone

Name

Address

Phone

Name

Address

Phone

T

Name _____
Address _____
_____
Phone _____

Name _____
Address _____
_____
Phone _____

Name _____
Address _____
_____
Phone _____

Name _____
Address _____
_____
Phone _____

Name _____
Address _____
_____
Phone _____

T

Name _____

Address _____

_____

Phone _____

Name _____

Address _____

_____

Phone _____

Name _____

Address _____

_____

Phone _____

Name _____

Address _____

_____

Phone _____

Name _____

Address _____

_____

Phone _____

Greenhouse Poinsettia.

*W*hat else is nature but God?

Seneca

U

Name

Address

Phone

Name

Address

Phone

Name

Address

Phone

Name

Address

Phone

Name

Address

Phone

U

Name

Address

Phone

Name

Address

Phone

Name

Address

Phone

Name

Address

Phone

Name

Address

Phone

U

Name

Address

Phone

Name

Address

Phone

Name

Address

Phone

Name

Address

Phone

Name

Address

Phone

Cedar of Lebanon trees near the South Transept.

V

Name
Address

Phone

Name
Address

Phone

Name
Address

Phone

Name
Address

Phone

Name
Address

Phone

V

Name _____
Address _____
_____
Phone _____

Name _____
Address _____
_____
Phone _____

Name _____
Address _____
_____
Phone _____

Name _____
Address _____
_____
Phone _____

Name _____
Address _____
_____
Phone _____

V

Name

Address

Phone

Name

Address

Phone

Name

Address

Phone

Name

Address

Phone

Name

Address

Phone

Ice-covered spring buds.

Name _____
Address _____
_____
Phone _____

Name _____
Address _____
_____
Phone _____

Name _____
Address _____
_____
Phone _____

Name _____
Address _____
_____
Phone _____

Name _____
Address _____
_____
Phone _____

Name _____
Address _____
_____
Phone _____

Name _____
Address _____
_____
Phone _____

Name _____
Address _____
_____
Phone _____

Name _____
Address _____
_____
Phone _____

Name _____
Address _____
_____
Phone _____

W

Name

Address

Phone

Name

Address

Phone

Name

Address

Phone

Name

Address

Phone

Name

Address

Phone

"Peace" Rose in the Herb Bed.

*O*ne touch of nature makes the whole world kin.

William Shakespeare

Name

Address

Phone

Name

Address

Phone

Name

Address

Phone

Name

Address

Phone

Name

Address

Phone

X-Y-Z

Name _____
Address _____
_____
Phone _____

Name _____
Address _____
_____
Phone _____

Name _____
Address _____
_____
Phone _____

Name _____
Address _____
_____
Phone _____

Name _____
Address _____
_____
Phone _____

X-Y-Z

Name

Address

Phone

Name

Address

Phone

Name

Address

Phone

Name

Address

Phone

Name

Address

Phone

Birthdays

January

February

March

April

May

June

Birthdays

July

August

September

October

November

December

Golden Chain Trees outside the Shadow House.

*What is Heaven? Is it not
Just a friendly garden plot,
Walled with stone and roofed with sun,
Where the days pass one by one,
Not too fast and not too slow,
Looking backward as they go
At the beauties left behind…*

Bliss Carman